When My Brother
Was an Aztec

When My Brother Was an Aztec

NATALIE DIAZ

COPPER CANYON PRESS

PORT TOWNSEND, WASHINGTON

Copper Canyon Press is in residence at Fort Worden State Park in Port Townsend, Washington, under the auspices of Centrum. Centrum is a gathering place for artists and creative thinkers from around the world, students of all ages and backgrounds, and audiences seeking extraordinary cultural enrichment.

LIBRARY OF CONGRESS CATALOGING-IN-PUBLICATION DATA

Diaz, Natalie.
 When my brother was an Aztec / Natalie Diaz.
   p. cm.
 ISBN 978-1-55659-383-3 (pbk. : alk. paper)
 I. Title.
 PS3604.I186W47 2012
 811'.6—DC23
                        2011052376

COPPER CANYON PRESS

Post Office Box 271

Port Townsend, Washington 98368

www.coppercanyonpress.org

Grateful acknowledgement is made to the editors of the books and periodicals in which these poems first appeared: "Why I Don't Mention Flowers When Conversations with My Brother Reach Uncomfortable Silences" in *Best New Poets 2007* and *The Southeast Review*; "How to Go to Dinner with a Brother on Drugs," "The Gospel of Guy No-Horse," "The Last Mojave Indian Barbie," "Reservation Mary," and "Tortilla Smoke: a Genesis" in *Black Renaissance Noire;* "Lorca's Red Dresses" in *Cider Press Review;* "Apotheosis of Kiss" in *Crab Orchard Review*; "Dome Riddle," "Reservation Grass," and "Self Portrait as a Chimera" in *Drunken Boat*; "As a Consequence of My Brother Stealing All the Lightbulbs," "Downhill Triolets," "I Lean Out the Window and She Nods Off in Bed, the Needle Gently Rocking on the Bedside Table," "Mariposa Nocturna," "Soirée Fantastique," "Toward the Amaranth Gates of War or Love," and "When the Beloved Asks, 'What Would You Do If You Woke Up and I Was a Shark?'" in *Narrative*; "My Brother At 3 A.M.," "No More Cake Here," "The Elephants," and "When My Brother Was an Aztec" in *Nimrod International Journal*; "Abecedarian Requiring Further Examination of Anglikan Seraphym Subjugation of a Wild Indian Rezervation" in *North American Review;* "Hand-Me-Down Halloween," "I Watch Her Eat the Apple," "If Eve Side-Stealer and Mary Busted-Chest Ruled the World," and "Métis," now titled "The Red Blues," in *Prairie Schooner;* "Black Magic Brother" and "Why I Hate Raisins" in *Sing: Poetry from the Indigenous Americas*; "The Wild Life Zoo" in Winning Writers.

Thank you to Khadijah Queen, Lee Quinby, and the Courting Risk
Reading Series; Carol Spaulding-Kruse, Jennifer Perrine, and the
Drake University Writers and Critics Series; Rosemary Catacalos,
Anisa Onofre, and Gemini Ink; Idyllwild Arts Academy; Fran
Ringold and the *Nimrod* staff; and the Old Dominion Creative
Writing Department for providing opportunities that were
important to developing this manuscript.

Thank you to Michael Wiegers and Copper Canyon Press for the
opportunity to publish my first book.

I am lucky to count many good people as my family and friends,
and I am grateful for their support of my work. I am indebted to
the generosity that has been shown to me on so many occasions.

With immeasurable gratitude to Cecilia, Diane, Eloise, Janet, and Ted

No hay mal que dure cien años,

ni cuerpo que lo resista.

—Spanish proverb

CONTENTS

When My Brother Was an Aztec

he lived in our basement and sacrificed my parents
      every morning. It was awful. Unforgivable. But they kept coming
          back for more. They loved him, was all they could say.

It started with him stumbling along *la Avenida de los Muertos,*
      my parents walking behind like effigies in a procession
          he might burn to the ground at any moment. They didn't know

what else to do except be there to pick him up when he died.
      They forgot who was dying, who was already dead. My brother
          quit wearing shirts when a carnival of dirty-breasted women

made him their leader, following him up and down the stairs—
      They were acrobats, moving, twitching like snakes— They fed him
          crushed diamonds and fire. He gobbled the gifts. My parents

begged him to pluck their eyes out. He thought he was
      Huitzilopochtli, a god, half-man half-hummingbird. My parents
          at his feet, wrecked honeysuckles, he lowered his swordlike mouth,

gorged on them, draining color until their eyebrows whitened.
      My brother shattered and quartered them before his basement festivals—
          waved their shaking hearts in his fists,

while flea-ridden dogs ran up and down the steps, licking their asses,
      turning tricks. Neighbors were amazed my parents' hearts kept
          growing back— It said a lot about my parents, or parents' hearts.

My brother flung them into *cenotes,* dropped them from cliffs,
      punched holes into their skulls like useless jars or vases,
          broke them to pieces and fed them to gods ruling

the ratty crotches of street fair whores with pocked faces
　　　　spreading their thighs in flophouses with no electricity. He slept
　　　　　　　in filthy clothes smelling of rotten peaches and matches, fell in love

with sparkling spoonfuls the carnival dog-women fed him. My parents
　　　　lost their appetites for food, for sons. Like all bad kings, my brother
　　　　　　　wore a crown, a green baseball cap turned backwards

with a Mexican flag embroidered on it. When he wore it
　　　　in the front yard, which he treated like his personal *zócalo,*
　　　　　　　all his realm knew he had the power that day, had all the jewels

a king could eat or smoke or shoot. The slave girls came
　　　　to the fence and ate out of his hands. He fed them *maíz*
　　　　　　　through the chain links. My parents watched from the window,

crying over their house turned zoo, their son who was
　　　　now a rusted cage. The Aztec held court in a salt cedar grove
　　　　　　　across the street where peacocks lived. My parents crossed fingers

so he'd never come back, lit *novena* candles
　　　　so he would. He always came home with turquoise and jade
　　　　　　　feathers and stinking of peacock shit. My parents gathered

what he'd left of their bodies, trying to stand without legs,
　　　　trying to defend his blows with missing arms, searching for their fingers
　　　　　　　to pray, to climb out of whatever dark belly my brother, the Aztec,
　　　　　　　　　their son, had fed them to.

I

Abecedarian Requiring Further Examination of Anglikan Seraphym Subjugation of a Wild Indian Rezervation

Angels don't come to the reservation.
Bats, maybe, or owls, boxy mottled things.
Coyotes, too. They all mean the same thing—
death. And death
eats angels, I guess, because I haven't seen an angel
fly through this valley ever.
Gabriel? Never heard of him. Know a guy named Gabe though—
he came through here one powwow and stayed, typical
Indian. Sure he had wings,
jailbird that he was. He flies around in stolen cars. Wherever he stops,
kids grow like gourds from women's bellies.
Like I said, no Indian I've ever heard of has ever been or seen an angel.
Maybe in a Christmas pageant or something—
Nazarene church holds one every December,
organized by Pastor John's wife. It's no wonder
Pastor John's son is the angel—everyone knows angels are white.
Quit bothering with angels, I say. They're no good for Indians.
Remember what happened last time
some white god came floating across the ocean?
Truth is, there may be angels, but if there are angels
up there, living on clouds or sitting on thrones across the sea wearing
velvet robes and golden rings, drinking whiskey from silver cups,
we're better off if they stay rich and fat and ugly and
'xactly where they are—in their own distant heavens.
You better hope you never see angels on the rez. If you do, they'll be
        marching you off to
Zion or Oklahoma, or some other hell they've mapped out for us.

Hand-Me-Down Halloween

The year we moved off / the reservation /
a / white / boy up the street gave me a green trash bag
fat with corduroys, bright collared shirts

& a two-piece / Tonto / costume
turquoise thunderbird on the chest
shirt & pants

the color of my grandmother's skin / reddish brown /
my mother's skin / brown-redskin /
My mother's boyfriend laughed

said now I was a / fake / Indian
look-it her now yer / In-din / girl is a / fake / In-din
My first Halloween off / the reservation /

/ white / Jeremiah told all his / white / friends
that I was wearing his old costume
/ A hand-me-down? /

I looked at my hands
All them / whites / laughed at me
/ called me half-breed /

threw Tootsie Rolls at / the half-breed / me
Later / darker / in the night
at / white / Jeremiah's front door / *tricker treat* /

I made a / good / little Injun his father said
now don't you make a / good / little Injun
He gave me a Tootsie Roll

More night came / darker / darker /
Mothers gathered their / white / kids from the dark
My / dark / mother gathered / empty / cans

while I waited to gather my / white / kid
I waited to gather / white / Jeremiah
He was / the skeleton / walking past my house

a glowing skull and ribs
I ran & tackled his / white / bones / in the street
His candy spilled out / like a million pinto beans /

Asphalt tore my / brown-red-skin / knees
I hit him harder and harder / whiter / and harder
He cried for his momma

I put my fist-me-downs / again and again and down /
He cried / for that white / She came running
She swung me off him

dug nails into my wrist
pulled me to my front door
yelled at her / white / kid to go wait at home

go wait at home Jeremiah, Momma will take care of this
She was ready / to take care of this /
to pound on my door / but no *tricker treat* /

My door was already open
and before that white could speak or knock
/ or put her hands down on my door /

my mother told her to take her hands off of me
taker / fuck-king / hands off my girl
My mother stepped / or fell / toward that white /

I don't remember what happened next
I don't remember that / white / momma leaving
/ but I know she did /

My mother's boyfriend said
well / Kemosabe / you ruined your costume
wull / Ke-mo-sa-be / you fuckt up yer costume

My first Halloween
off / the reservation /
my mother said / maybe / next year

you can be a little Tinker Bell / or something /
now go git that / white / boy's can-dee
—iss-in the road

Why I Hate Raisins

And is it only the mouth and belly which are
injured by hunger and thirst?

Mencius

Love is a pound of sticky raisins
packed tight in black and white
government boxes the day we had no
groceries. I told my mom I was hungry.
She gave me the whole bright box.
USDA stamped like a fist on the side.
I ate them all in ten minutes. Ate
too many too fast. It wasn't long
before those old grapes set like black
clay at the bottom of my belly
making it ache and swell.

I complained, *I hate raisins.*
I just wanted a sandwich like other kids.
Well that's all we've got, my mom sighed.
And what other kids?
Everyone but me, I told her.
She said, *You mean the white kids.*
You want to be a white kid?
Well too bad 'cause you're my kid.
I cried, *At least the white kids get a sandwich.*
At least the white kids don't get the shits.

That's when she slapped me. Left me
holding my mouth and stomach—
devoured by shame.

I still hate raisins,
but not for the crooked commodity lines
we stood in to get them—winding
around and in the tribal gymnasium.
Not for the awkward cardboard boxes
we carried them home in. Not for the shits
or how they distended my belly.
I hate raisins because now I know
my mom was hungry that day, too,
and I ate all the raisins.

The Red Blues

There is a dawn between my legs,
a rising of mad rouge birds, overflowing
and crazy-mean, bronze-tailed hawks,
a phoenix preening
sharp-hot wings, pretty pecking procession,
feathers flashing like flames
in a *Semana Santa* parade.

There are bulls between my legs,
a *torera*
stabbing her *banderillas*,
snapping her cape, tippy-toes scraping
my mottled thighs, the crowd's throats open,
shining like new scars, *cornadas* glowing
from beneath hands and white handkerchiefs
bright as bandages.

There are car wrecks between my legs,
a mess of maroon Volkswagens,
a rusted bus abandoned in the Grand Canyon,
a gas tanker in flames,
an IHS van full of corned beef hash,
an open can of commodity beets
on this village's one main road, a stoplight
pulsing like a bullet hole, a police car
flickering like a new scab,
an ambulance driven by Custer,
another ambulance
for Custer.

There is a war between my legs,
'ahway nyavay, a wager, a fight, a losing

that cramps my fists, a battle on eroding banks
of muddy creeks, the stench of metal,
purple-gray clotting the air,
in the grass the bodies
dim, cracked pomegranates, stone fruit,
this orchard stains
like a cemetery.

There is a martyr between my legs,
my personal San Sebastián
leaking reed arrows and sin, stubbornly sewing
a sacred red ribbon dress, *ahvay chuchqer,*
the carmine threads
pull the Colorado River, *'Aha Haviily,* clay,
and creosotes from the skirt,
each wound a week,
a coral moon, a calendar, a begging
for a master, or a slave, for a god
in magic cochineal pants.

There are broken baskets between my legs,
cracked vases, terra-cotta crumbs,
crippled grandmothers with mahogany skins
whose ruby shoes throb on shelves in closets,
who teach me to vomit
this fuchsia madness,
this scarlet smallpox blanket,
this sugar-riddled amputated robe,
these cursive curses scrawling down my calves,
this rotting strawberry field, swollen sunset,
hemoglobin joke with no punch line,
this crimson garbage truck,
this bloody nose, splintered cherry tree, *manzano,*

this *métis* Mary's heart,
guitarra acerezada, red race *mestiza,* this cattle train,
this hand-me-down adobe drum,
this slug in the mouth,
this *'av'unye 'ahwaatm, via roja dolorosa,*
this dark hut, this mud house, this dirty bed,
this period of exile.

The Gospel of Guy No-Horse

At The Injun That Could, a jalopy bar drooping and lopsided
on the bank of the Colorado River—a once mighty red body
now dammed and tamed blue—Guy No-Horse was glistening
drunk and dancing fancy with two white gals—both yellow-haired
tourists still in bikini tops, freckled skins blistered pink
by the savage Mohave Desert sun.

Though The Injun, as it was known by locals, had no true dance floor—
truths meant little on such a night—card tables covered in drink, ash,
and melting ice had been pushed aside, shoved together to make a place
for the rhythms that came easy to people in the coyote hours
beyond midnight.

In the midst of Camel smoke hanging lower and thicker
than a September monsoon, No-Horse rode high, his PIMC-issued
wheelchair transfigured—a magical chariot drawn by two blond,
beer-clumsy palominos perfumed with coconut sunscreen and dollar-fifty
Budweisers. He was as careful as any man could be at almost 2 a.m.
to avoid their sunburned toes—in the brown light of The Injun, chips
in their toenail polish glinted like diamonds.

Other Indians noticed the awkward trinity and gathered round
in a dented circle, clapping, whooping, slinging obscenities
from their tongues of fire: *Ya-ha! Ya-ha!* Jeering their dark horse,
No-Horse, toward the finish line of an obviously rigged race.

No-Horse didn't hear their rabble, which was soon overpowered
as the two-man band behind the bar really got after it—a jam
probably about love, but maybe about freedom, and definitely
about him, as his fair-haired tandem, his denim-skirted pendulums
kept time. The time being now—

No-Horse sucked his lips, imagined the taste of the white girls'
thrusting hips. *Hey!* He sang. *Hey!* He smiled. *Hey!* He spun around
in the middle of a crowd of his fellow tribesmen, a sparkling centurion
moving as fluid as an Indian could be at almost two in the morning,
rolling back, forth, popping wheelies that tipped his big head
and swung his braids like shiny lassos of lust. The two white gals
looked down at him, looked back up at each other, raised their plastic
Solo cups-runneth-over, laughing loudly, hysterical at the very thought
of dancing with a broken-down Indian.

But about that laughter, No-Horse didn't give a damn.
This was an edge of rez where warriors were made on nights
like these, with music like this, and tonight he was out, dancing
at The Injun That Could. If you'd seen the lightning of his smile,
not the empty space leaking from his thighs, you might have believed
that man was walking on water, or at least that he had legs again.

And as for the white girls slurring around him like two bedraggled
angels, one holding on to the handle of his wheelchair, the other
spilling her drink all down the front of her shirt, well, for them
he was sorry. Because this was not a John Wayne movie,
this was The Injun That Could, and the only cavalry riding this night
was in No-Horse's veins. *Hey! Hey! Hey!* he hollered.

A Woman with No Legs

for Lona Barrackman

Plays solitaire on TV trays with decks of old casino cards   Trades
her clothes for faded nightgowns long & loose like ghosts   Drinks
water & Diet Coke from blue cups with plastic bendy straws   Bathes
twice a week   Is dropped to the green tiles of her HUD home while
her daughters try to change her sheets & a child watches through
a crack in the door   Doesn't attend church services cakewalks or
Indian Days parades   Slides her old shoes under the legs of wooden
tables & chairs   Lives years & years in beds & wheelchairs stamped
"Needles Hospital" in white stencil   Dreams of playing kick-the-
can in asphalt cul-de-sacs below the brown hum of streetlights about
to burn out   Asks her great-grandchildren to race from one end of
her room to the other as fast as they can & the whole time she whoops
Faster! Faster!   Can't remember doing jackknifes or cannonballs
or breaking the surface of the Colorado River   Can't forget being
locked in closets at the old Indian school   Still cries telling how
she peed the bed there   How the white teacher wrapped her in her
wet sheets & made her stand in the hall all day for the other Indian
kids to see   Receives visits from Nazarene preachers Contract
Health & Records nurses & medicine men from Parker who knock
stones & sticks together & spit magic saliva over her   Taps out
the two-step rhythm of Bird dances with her fingers   Curses in
Mojave some mornings   Prays in English most nights   Told me
to keep my eyes open for the white man named Diabetes who is out
there somewhere carrying her legs in red biohazard bags tucked
under his arms   Asks me to rub her legs which aren't there so I
pretend by pressing my hands into the empty sheets at the foot of
her bed   Feels she's lost part of her memory the part the legs knew
best like earth   Her missing kneecaps are bright bones caught in
my throat

Tortilla Smoke: A Genesis

In the beginning, light was shaved from its cob,
white kernels divided from dark ones, put to the pestle
until each sparked like a star. By nightfall, tortillas sprang up
from the dust, billowed like a fleet of prairie schooners
sailing a flat black sky, moons hot white
on the blue-flamed stove of the earth, and they were good.

Some tortillas wandered the dry ground
like bright tribes, others settled through the floury ceiling
el cielo de mis sueños, hovering above our tents,
over our beds—floppy white Frisbees, spinning, whirling
like project merry-go-rounds—they were fruitful and multiplied,
subduing all the beasts, eyeteeth, and bellies of the world.

How we prayed to the tortilla god: to roll us up
like burritos—tight and fat *como porros*—to hold us
in His lips, to be ignited, lit up luminous with Holy Spirit
dancing on the edge of a table, grooving all up and down
the gold piping of the green robe of San Peregrino—
the saint who keeps the black spots away,

to toke and be token, carried up up
away in tortilla smoke, up to the steeple
where the angels and our grandpas live
      porque nuestras madres nos dijeron que viven allí—
high to the top that is the bottom, the side, the side,
the space between, back to the end that is the beginning—

a giant ball of *masa* rolling, rolling, rolling down,
riding hard the arc of earth—gathering rocks, size, lemon
trees, Joshua trees, creosotes, size, spray-painted
blue bicycles rusting in gardens, hunched bow-legged grandpas in white

undershirts that cover cancers whittling their organs like thorns
and thistles, like dark eyes wide open, like sin—leaving behind
bits and pieces of finger-sticky dough grandmas mistake
for Communion *y toman la hostia*—it clings to their ribs
like gum they swallowed in first grade.

The grandmas return from *misa,* with full to the brim
estómagos and overflowing souls, to empty homes.
They tie on their aprons. Between their palms they sculpt and caress,
stroke and press, dozens and dozens of tortillas—stack them
from basement to attic, from wall to wall, crowding closets,
jamming drawers, filling cupboards and *el vacío.*

At night they kiss ceramic statues of Virgin Marys,
roll rosary beads between their index fingers and thumbs,
weep tears prettier than holy water—
  sana sana colita de rana si no sanas ahora sanarás mañana—
When they wake they realize frogs haven't had tails in ages,
they hope gravity doesn't last long, and they wait—
y esperan y esperan y esperamos—to be carried up up—anywhere—
on round white magic carpets and tortilla smoke.

Reservation Mary

Mary Lambert was born at the Indian hospital on the rez.
She never missed a 3-pointer in the first thirteen years of her life.
She started smoking pot in seventh grade, still, never missed
a 3-pointer, but eventually missed most of her freshman classes
and finally dropped out of high school.

A year or so later, a smooth-faced Mojave who had a jump shot
smoother than a silver can of commodity shortening and soared
for rebounds like he was made of red-tailed hawk feathers
visited her rez for a money tournament. His team won the money,
and he won MVI—Most Valuable Indian.

Afterward, at the little bar on the corner of Indian Route 1,
where the only people not allowed to drink were dialysis patients,
he told Mary she was his favorite, his first string,
that he'd dropped all those buckets for her. He spent his entire cut
of the tournament winnings on her Wild Turkey 'n' Cokes,
told her he was going to stay the night with her, even though
it was already morning when they stumbled from the bar.

He stayed and stayed and stayed, then left—
her heart felt pierced with spears and arrows, and her belly swelled
round as an August melon.

That was a lifetime ago. Now, she's seventeen. She kept the baby
and the weight and sells famous frybread and breakfast burritos
at tribal entities on pay days—tortillas round and chewy as Communion
wafers embracing commod cheese and government potatoes,
delivered in tinfoil from the trunk of an old brown Buick
with a cracked windshield and a pair of baby Jordan shoes hanging
from the rearview mirror—her sleeping brown baby tied tightly
into a cradleboard in the backseat.

Just the other day, at a party on first beach, someone asked
if she still had that 3-point touch, if she wished she still played ball,
and she answered that she wished a lot of things,
but what she wished for most at that minute was that she could turn
the entire Colorado River into E & J Ripple—
she went on a beer run instead,
and as she made her way over the bumpy back roads along the river,
that smooth-faced baby in the backseat cried out for something.

Cloud Watching

Betsy Ross needled hot stars to Mr. Washington's bedspread—
    they weren't hers to give. So, when the cavalry came,
        we ate their horses. Then, unfortunately, our bellies were filled
        with bullet holes.

Pack the suitcases with white cans of corned beef—
    when we leave, our hunger will go with us,
        following behind, a dog with ribs like a harp.

Blue gourds glow and rattle like a two-man band:
    Hotchkiss on backup vocals and Gatling on drums.
        The rhythm is set by our boys dancing the warpath—
            the meth 3-step. Grandmothers dance their legs off—
        who now will teach us to stand?

We carry dimming lamps like god cages—
    they help us to see that it is dark. In the dark our hands
        pretend to pray but really make love.
        Soon we'll give birth to fists—they'll open up
            black eyes and split grins—we'll all cry out.

History has chapped lips, unkissable lips—
    he gave me a coral necklace that shines bright as a chokehold.
        He gives and gives—census names given to Mojaves:
            George and Martha Washington, Abraham Lincoln,
            Robin Hood, Rip Van Winkle.

Loot bag ghosts float fatly in dark museum corners—
    I see my grandfather's flutes and rabbit sticks in their guts.
        About the beautiful dresses emptied of breasts...
            they were nothing compared to the emptied bodies.

Splintering cradleboards sing bone lullabies—
  they hush the mention of half-breed babies buried or left on riverbanks.
   When you ask about officers who chased our screaming women
    into the arrowweeds, they only hum.

A tongue will wrestle its mouth to death and lose—
  language is a cemetery.
   Tribal dentists light lab-coat pyres in memoriam of lost molars—
    our cavities are larger than HUD houses.
     Some Indians' wisdom teeth never stop growing back in—
    we were made to bite back—
     until we learn to bite first.

Mercy Songs to Melancholy

It's the things I might have said that fester.
Clemence Dane

I found your blue suitcases
in my little sister's closet,
navy socks with holes in the heels, packets of black
poplar seeds, damp underwear.
Please hang your charcoal three-piece suit somewhere
else. Please stop
dragging wire hangers across her arms and stomach.

~

Who mines her throat?
The picks spark, sparklers from a Fourth of July
when stars weren't bits of glass.
The clanking is too many
pennies in each pocket
on a riverbank, telephones and wrong numbers.
Why won't you put her on the phone? Why
did you cover the bedroom windows with yesterday's
newspaper? The pages are yellow,
the stories are old.

~

There's no such thing as gentle weeping.
Your gray guitar
is my sister—the hole in the chest
gives you both away.

~

I've seen you before
in the Picasso museum—all corners,
        a plaza of bulls, *banderillas*. The grandstand full.
Old women, sisters begging for ears and tails, shaking
handkerchiefs—in the sky, glittering magpies,
razorblade ballads, and Ma Rainey records. These blues are
        not so sweet as jelly beans. They are not small.

                        ~

        She is my sister, goddammit.
        She is too young to sit at your table,
        to eat from your dark pie.

If Eve Side-Stealer
& Mary Busted-Chest
Ruled the World

What if Eve was an Indian
& Adam was never kneaded
from the earth, Eve *was* Earth
& ribs were her idea all along?

What if Mary was an Indian
& when Gabriel visited her wigwam
she was away at a monthly WIC clinic
receiving eggs, boxed cheese
& peanut butter instead of Jesus?

What if God was an Indian
with turquoise wings & coral breasts
who invented a game called White Man Chess
played on silver boards with all white pieces
pawns & kings & only one side, the white side
& the more they won the more they were beaten?

What if the world was an Indian
whose head & back were flat from being strapped
to a cradleboard as a baby & when she slept
she had nightmares lit up by yellow-haired men & ships
scraping anchors in her throat? What if she wailed
all night while great waves rose up carrying the fleets
across her flat back, over the edge of the flat world?

The Last Mojave Indian Barbie

Wired to her display box were a pair of one-size-fits-all-Indians stiletto moccasins, faux turquoise earrings, a dream catcher, a copy of *Indian Country Today*, erasable markers for chin and forehead tattoos, and two six-packs of mini magic beer bottles—when tilted up, the bottles turned clear, when turned right-side-up, the bottles refilled. Mojave Barbie repeatedly drank Ken and Skipper under their pink plastic patio table sets. Skipper said she drank like a boy.

Mojave Barbie secretly hated the color of her new friends' apricot skins, how they burned after riding in Ken's convertible Camaro with the top down, hated how their micro hairbrushes tangled and knotted in her own thick, black hair, which they always wanted to braid. There wasn't any diet cola in their cute little ice chests, and worst of all, Mojave Barbie couldn't find a single soft spot on her body to inject her insulin. It had taken years of court cases, litigation, letters from tribal council members, testimonials from CHR nurses, and a few diabetic comas just to receive permission to buy the never-released hypodermic needle accessory kit—before that, she'd bought most on the Japanese black market—Mattel didn't like toying around with the possibility of a Junkie Barbie.

Mojave Barbie had been banned from the horse stables and was no longer invited to dinner, not since she let it slip that when the cavalry came to Fort Mojave, the Mojaves ate a few horses. It had happened, and she only let it slip after Skipper tried to force her to admit the Mojave Creation was just a myth: *It's true. I'm from Spirit Mountain*, Mojave Barbie had said. *No, you're not*, Skipper had argued. *You came from Asia*. But Mojave Barbie wasn't missing much—they didn't have lazy man's bread or tortillas in the Barbie Stovetop to Tabletop Deluxe Kitchen. In fact, they only had a breakfast set, so they ate the same two sunny-side-up eggs and pancakes every meal.

Each night after dinner, Mojave Barbie sneaked from the guesthouse—next to the tennis courts and Hairtastic Salon—to rendezvous with Ken, sometimes in the collapsible Glamour Camper, but most often in the Dream Pool. She would *yenni* Ken all night long. (*Yenni* was the Mojave word for sex, explained a culturally informative booklet included in Mojave Barbie's box, along with an authentic frybread recipe, her Certificate of Indian Blood, a casino player's card, and a voided per capita check.) They took precautions to prevent waking others inside the Dream House—Mojave Barbie's tan webbed hand covering Ken's always-open mouth muffled his ejaculations.

One night, after drinking a pint of Black Velvet disguised as a bottle of suntan lotion, Ken felt especially playful. Ken was wild, wanted to sport his plastic Stetson and pleather holsters, wanted Mojave Barbie to wear her traditional outfit, still twist-tied to her box. She agreed and donned her mesquite-bark skirt and went shirtless except for strands of blue and white glass beads that hung down in coils around her neck. The single feather in her hair tickled Ken's fancy. He begged Mojave Barbie to wrap her wide, dark hips around him in the "Mojave Death Grip," an indigenous love maneuver that made him thankful for his double-jointed pelvis. (A Mojave Death Grip Graphic How-To Manual was once included in the culturally informative booklet, but a string of disjointed legs and a campaign by the Girl Scouts of America led to a recall.) Ken pointed his wooden six-shooter and chased her up the Dream Slide. The weight of the perfectly proportioned bodies sent the pool accessory crashing to the patio. Every light in every window painted itself on as the Dream House swung open from the middle, giving all inside a sneak peek at naked Ken's hard body and naked Mojave Barbie gripping his pistol, both mid-yenni and dripping wet.

Ken was punished by Mattel's higher-ups, had his tennis racket, tuxedo, Limited Edition Hummer, scuba and snorkel gear, aviator sunglasses, Harley, windjammer sailboard, his iPad and iPhone confiscated. Mojave Barbie had been caught red-handed and bare-breasted. She was being relocated—a job dealing blackjack at some California casino. On her way out the gate, she kicked the plastic cocker spaniel, which fell sideways but never pulled its tongue in or even barked—she felt an ache behind her 39 EE left breast for her rez dog, which had been discontinued long ago. Mojave Barbie tossed a trash bag filled with clothes and accessories into her primered Barbie Happy Family Volvo, which she'd bought at a yard sale. The car had hidden beneath a tarp in the Dream House driveway since she got there. She climbed through the passenger door over to the driver's seat, an explosion of ripped vinyl, towels, and duct tape. She pumped and pumped the gas pedal, clicked and clicked the ignition, until the jalopy fired up. Mojave Barbie rolled away, her mismatched hubcaps wobbling and rattling, a book of yellow WIC coupons rustling on the dash, and a Joy Harjo tape melted in the tape deck blaring, *I'm not afraid to be hungry. I'm not afraid to be full.*

Mom and Dad Barbie, Grandma Barbie, Skipper, and Ken stood on the Dream House balcony and watched Mojave Barbie go. Grandma Barbie tilted at the waist whispering to Mom Barbie, *They should've kept that one in the cupboard.* Dad Barbie piped in, *Yep, it's always a gamble with those people.* Mom Barbie was silent, hoping the purpling, bruise-like marks the size of mouths circling Ken's neck were not what she thought they were: hickies, or, as the culturally informative booklet explained, a "Mojave necklace." Skipper complained to Ken that Mojave Barbie had flipped them off as she drove out the wrought-iron gates, which, of course, locked behind her with a clang. Ken fingered the blue bead in his pocket and reassured Skipper, *Mojave Barbie was probably waving goodbye—with hands like that, you can never be sure.*

Reservation Grass

I keep no account with lamentation
Walt Whitman

We smoke more grass than we ever promise to plant.
Our front yards are green and brown, triangles of glass—*What is the*
　　grass?—emeralds and garnets sewed like seeds in the dirt.
The shards of glass grow men bunched together—*multitudes*—men larger
　　than weeds and Whitmans, leaning against the sides of houses—
　　dance with the dancers and drink with the drinkers—upon dirt not
　　lawn.

Corned beef comes on the first of every month—*this the meat of hunger*—
　　in white cans with bold black writing.
We—*myself and mine*—toss it in a pot and wonder how it will ever feed
　　us all—*witness and wait*—but never worry, never fret, never give a
　　damn, over mowing the grass.

What have we—*the red aborigines*—out of hopeful green stuff woven?

Other Small Thundering

We are born with spinning coins in place of eyes,
paid in full to ferry Charon's narrow skiffs—
    we red-cloaked captains helming dizzying fits
    of sleep. Tied to the masts,
not to be driven mad by the caroling of thirsty children
or the symphony of dogs slaking hunger
by licking our ribcages like xylophones.
Our medicine bags are anchored with buffalo nickels—
    sleek skulls etched by Gatlings.
How we plow and furrow the murky Styx, lovingly
digging with smooth dark oars—
    like they are Grandmother's missing legs—
        a familiar throb of kneecap, shin, ankle, foot—
    promising to carry us home.

A gunnysack full of tigers wrestles in our chests—
    they pace, stalking our hearts, building a jail
    with their stripes. Each tail a fuse. Each eye a cinder.
Chest translates to bomb.
Bomb is a song—
    the drum's shame-hollowed lament.
Burlap is no place for prayers or hands.
The reservation is no place for a jungle.
    But our stomachs growl. Somewhere within us
    there lies a king, and when we find him…

The snow-dim prairies are garlanded with children—
    my people fancy dance circles around pyres but do not
    celebrate the bodies, small, open, red as hollyhocks.
Some crawled until they came undone—
    petal by petal,

striping the white field crimson.
Others lay where they first fell, enamored by the warmth
of a blanket of blood.
My dress is bluer than a sky weeping bones—
    so this is the way to build a flag—
        with a pretty little Springfield .45 caliber rifle.
    So this is the way to sew wounds—
        with a hot little Howitzer.

Yesterday is much closer than today—
    a black bayonet carried between the shoulder blades
    like an itch or the bud of a wing.
We've memorized the way a Hotchkiss can wreck a mouth.
Streetlights glow, neon gourds, electric dandelions—
    blow them out!
Wish hard for orange buttes and purple canyons,
moon-hoofed horses with manes made from wars,
other small thundering.

Jimmy Eagle's Hot Cowboy Boots Blues

> *On June 26, 1975, two FBI agents drove into the*
> *Jumping Bull property on the Sioux Reservation,*
> *allegedly in pursuit of Jimmy Eagle, a teen*
> *accused of stealing a pair of cowboy boots.*

Jimmy Eagle, them FBI boys are just a-throbbin' for you
    since you put on them pretty red-handed hot cowboy boots

Better hope your red pickup grows wings and flies fast
    'cause Uncle Sam's dreamin' down Injuns in red Dakota grass

The crime's not so much, but they don't belong to you
    What's a wild bird like you need with whiteman shoes?

Yep, Jimbo, the feds have a warrant named "you"
    Soar Jumping Bull's golden hills, boy, and defend your coup

Jimmy Eagle, the brass is straight-lampin' for you
    They're hot and you're red-handed with 'em sharp cowboy boots

The crime's not so much, but they don't belong to you
    What's a wild bird like you need with whiteman shoes?

Now, Jimmy, they're callin' in cavalry ghosts of the past
    Head for the stockpiled commods and arrows, man, hope that they last

Jimmy, baby, the gov'ments on your tail with a green light to shoot
    worked-up 'n' tizzied for some hot goddamn red-handed cowboy boots

The crime's not so much, but they don't belong to you
    What's a wild bird like you need with whiteman shoes?

Go 'head, Jimmy, stomp them new shoes, dance up the sand, make 'em flash
    'cause they're lookin' to bury bullets in your brown barefoot ass

The Facts of Art

woven plaque basket with sunflower design, Hopi,
Arizona, before 1935

from an American Indian basketry exhibit in
Portsmouth, Virginia

The Arizona highway sailed across the desert—
   a gray battleship drawing a black wake,
      halting at the foot of the orange mesa,
         unwilling to go around.

Hopi men and women—brown, and small, and claylike
   —peered down from their tabletops at yellow tractors, water trucks,
      and white men blistered with sun—red as fire ants—towing
         sunscreen-slathered wives in glinting Airstream trailers
      in caravans behind them.

Elders knew these BIA roads were bad medicine—knew too
   that young men listen less and less, and these young Hopi men
      needed work, hence set aside their tools, blocks of cottonwood root
         and half-finished Koshari the clown katsinas, then
            signed on with the Department of Transportation,

were hired to stab drills deep into the earth's thick red flesh
   on First Mesa, drive giant sparking blades across the mesas' faces,
      run the drill bits so deep they smoked, bearding all the Hopi men
         in white—*Bad spirits,* said the Elders—

The blades caught fire, burned out—*Ma'saw is angry,* the Elders said.
   New blades were flown in by helicopter. While Elders dreamed
      their arms and legs had been cleaved off and their torsos were flung
         over the edge of a dinner table, the young Hopi men went
            back to work cutting the land into large chunks of rust.

Nobody noticed at first—not the white workers,
　　　not the Indian workers—but in the mounds of dismantled mesa,
　　　　　among the clods and piles of sand,
　　　　　　　lay the small gray bowls of babies' skulls.

Not until they climbed to the bottom did they see
　　　the silvered bones glinting from the freshly sliced dirt-and-rock wall—
　　　　　a mausoleum mosaic, a sick tapestry: the tiny remains
　　　　　　　roused from death's dusty cradle, cut in half, cracked,
　　　　　　　　　wrapped in time-tattered scraps of blankets.

Let's call it a day, the white foreman said.
　　　That night, all the Indian workers got sad-drunk—got sick
　　　　　—while Elders sank to their kivas in prayer. Next morning,
　　　　　　　as dawn festered on the horizon, state workers scaled the mesas,
　　　　　　　　　knocked at the doors of pueblos that had them, hollered
　　　　　　　　　into those without them,

demanding the Hopi men come back to work—then begging them—
　　　then buying them whiskey—begging again—finally sending their white
　　　　　wives up the dangerous trail etched into the steep sides
　　　　　　　to buy baskets from Hopi wives and grandmothers
　　　　　　　　　as a sign of treaty.

When that didn't work, the state workers called the Indians lazy,
　　　sent their sunhat-wearing wives back up to buy more baskets—
　　　　　katsinas too　　then called the Hopis *good-for-nothings,*
　　　　　　　before begging them back once more.

We'll try again in the morning, the foreman said.
　　　But the Indian workers never returned—
　　　　　The BIA's and DOT's calls to work went unanswered,
　　　　　　　as the fevered Hopis stayed huddled inside.

The small bones half-buried in the crevices of mesa—
    in the once-holy darkness of silent earth and always-night—
        smiled or sighed beneath the moonlight, while white women
      in Airstream trailers wrote letters home

praising their husbands' patience, describing the lazy savages:
    such squalor in their stone and plaster homes—cobs of corn stacked
        floor to ceiling against crumbling walls—their devilish ceremonies
      and the barbaric way they buried their babies,
        oh, and those beautiful, beautiful baskets.

Prayers or Oubliettes

1

Despair has a loose daughter.
I lay with her and read the body's bones
like stories. I can tell you the year-long myth
of her hips, how I numbered stars,
the abacus of her mouth.

2

The sheets are berserk with wind's riddling.
All the beds of the past cannot dress the ghosts
at my table. Their breasts rest on plates
like broken goblets whose rims I once thirsted at.
Instead of grace, we rattle forks
in our empty bowls.

3

We are the muezzins of the desert
crying out like mockers from memory's
violet towers. We scour the earth
as Isis did. Fall is forever here—
women's dresses wrinkle
on the ground, men fall to their knees
in heaps, genitals rotting like spent fruit—
even our roots fall from the soil.

4

The world has tired of tears.
We weep owls now. They live longer.
They know their way in the dark.

5

Unfasten your cage of teeth and tongue.
The taste of a thousand moths is chalk.
The mottled wings are the words to pain.

6

We have no mazel tov.
We call out for our mothers
with empty wine jugs at our heels.

The Clouds Are Buffalo Limping toward Jesus

weeping   blooms

of   white

smoke.

II

My Brother at 3 A.M.

He sat cross-legged, weeping on the steps
when Mom unlocked and opened the front door.
>   *O God,* he said. *O God.*
>>   *He wants to kill me, Mom.*

When Mom unlocked and opened the front door
at 3 a.m., she was in her nightgown, Dad was asleep.
>   *He wants to kill me,* he told her,
>>   looking over his shoulder.

3 a.m. and in her nightgown, Dad asleep,
What's going on? she asked. *Who wants to kill you?*
>   He looked over his shoulder.
>>   *The devil does. Look at him, over there.*

She asked, *What are you on? Who wants to kill you?*
The sky wasn't black or blue but the green of a dying night.
>   *The devil, look at him, over there.*
>>   He pointed to the corner house.

The sky wasn't black or blue but the dying green of night.
Stars had closed their eyes or sheathed their knives.
>   My brother pointed to the corner house.
>>   His lips flickered with sores.

Stars had closed their eyes or sheathed their knives.
O God, I can see the tail, he said. *O God, look.*
>   Mom winced at the sores on his lips.
>>   *It's sticking out from behind the house.*

O God, see the tail, he said. *Look at the goddamned tail.*
He sat cross-legged, weeping on the front steps.

Mom finally saw it, a hellish vision, my brother.

O God, O God, she said.

Zoology

My father brought home a zebra from Sinaloa. *This house is a zoo,* my mother wept. *Ay, but this amazing creature is for you, mi vida,* he said. *You only give me beasts,* she sobbed, flinging herself over the bony, swayed back of the zebra. She loosened a new Colorado River of tears, so much water that the zebra's stripes melted and pooled at his ankles like four beaten prisoners. *Ay, you see,* my father howled, *you ruined it. Amor, it is no zebra. It is a burro painted like a zebra. But, don't be sad. The beasts are not beasts. They are our children painted like hyenas.*

We knew better. My mother had been weeping for one hundred years, and in all that time, our ghoulish mouths had grown redder, our beady eyes darker, and our wet teeth even longer. Faces she couldn't scrub from our heads. Tails that always grew back.

With one hundred years comes wisdom, and my mother was right. We are a zoo, and we will not spare even our parents the price of admission—they will pay to watch us eat *el burro*. My father will fall on his knees like a man who has just lost his zebra. My mother will paint the thin gray bars of a cage over her skin and reach out for us.

How to Go to Dinner with a Brother on Drugs

If he's wearing knives for eyes,
if he's dressed for a Day of the Dead parade—
three-piece skeleton suit, cummerbund of ribs—
his pelvic girdle will look like a Halloween mask.

The bones, he'll complain, make him itch. *Each ulna
a tingle.* His mandible might tickle.
If he cannot stop scratching, suggest that he change,
but not because he itches—do it for the scratching,
do it for the bones.

Okay, okay, he'll give in, *I'll change.*
He'll go back upstairs, and as he climbs away,
his back will be something else—one shoulder blade
a failed wing, the other a silver shovel.
He hasn't eaten in years. He will never change.

Be some kind of happy he didn't appear dressed
as a greed god—headdress of green quetzal feathers,
jaguar loincloth littered with bite-shaped rosettes—
because tonight you are not in the mood
to have your heart ripped out. It gets old,
having your heart ripped out,
being opened up that way.

Your brother will come back down again,
this time dressed as a Judas effigy.
I know, I know, he'll joke. *It's not Easter. So what?*
Be straight with him. Tell him the truth.
Tell him, *Judas had a rope around his neck.*
When he asks if an old lamp cord will do, just shrug.

He'll go back upstairs, and you will be there,
close enough to the door to leave, but you won't.
You will wait, unsure of what you are waiting for.

Wait for him in the living room
of your parents' home-turned-misery-museum.
Visit the perpetual exhibits: *Someone Is Tapping
My Phone, Como Deshacer a Tus Padres,
Jesus Told Me To,* and *Mon Frère*—
ten, twenty, forty dismantled phones dissected
on the dining table: glinting snarls of copper,
sheets of numbered buttons, small magnets,
jagged, ruptured shafts of lithium batteries,
empty 2-liters of Diet Coke with dirty tubing snaking
from the necks, shells of Ataris, radios, television sets,
and the Electrolux, all cracked open like dark nuts,
innards heaped across the floor.

And your pick for Best of Show:
Why Dad Can't Find the Lightbulbs—
a hundred glowing bells of gutted lightbulbs,
each rocking in a semicircle on the counter
beneath Mom's hanging philodendron.

Your parents' home will look like an al-Qaeda
yard sale. It will look like a bomb factory,
which might give you hope, if there were
such a thing. You are not so lucky—
there is no fuse here for you to find.

Not long ago, your brother lived with you.
You called it, *One last shot,* a three-quarter-court
heave, a buzzer-beater to win something of him back.
But who were you kidding? You took him in

with no grand dreams of salvation, but only to ease
the guilt of never having tried.

He spent his nights in your bathroom
with a turquoise BernzOmatic handheld propane torch,
a Merlin mixing magic, then shape-shifting into lions,
and tigers, and bears, *Oh fuck,* pacing your balcony
like Borges's blue tiger, fighting the cavalry in the moon,
conquering night with his blue flame, and plotting to steal
your truck keys, hidden under your pillow.
Finally, you found the nerve to ask him to leave,
so he took his propane torch and left you
with his meth pipe ringing in the dryer.

Now, he's fresh-released from Rancho Cucamonga—
having traveled the Mojave Trail in chains—
living with your parents, and you have come
to take him to dinner—because he is your brother,
because you heard he was cleaning up,
because dinner is a thing with a clear beginning
and end, a measured amount of time,
a ritual everyone knows, even your brother.
Sit down. Eat. Get up. Go home.

Holler upstairs to your brother to hurry.
He won't come right away.
Remember how long it took the Minotaur
to escape the labyrinth.

Your father will be in the living room, too,
sitting in a rocking chair in the dark,
wearing his *luchador* mask—he is El Santo.
His face is pale. His face is bone-white. His eyes

are hollow teardrops. His mouth a dark, *O*—
He is still surprised by what his life has become.

Don't dare think about unmasking your father.
His mask is the only fight he has left.
He is bankrupt of *planchas* and *topes*.
He has no more *huracanranas* to give.
Leave him to imagine himself jumping
over the top rope, out of the ring,
running off, his silver-masked head
cutting the night like a butcher knife.

When your brother finally appears,
the lamp cord knotted at his neck
should do the trick, so leave to the restaurant.
It will be hard to look at him in the truck,
dressed as a Judas effigy. Don't forget,
a single match could devour him like a neon
tooth, canopying him in a bright tent of pain—
press the truck's lighter into the socket.

Meth—his singing sirens, his jealous jinn
conjuring up sandstorms within him, his Harpy
harem—has sucked the beauty from his face.
He is a Cheshire cat, a gang of grins.
His new face all jaw, all smile and bite.

Look at your brother—he is Borges's bestiary.
He is a zoo of imaginary beings.

Your brother's jaw is a third passenger in the truck—
it flexes in the wind coming in through the window,
resetting and rehinging, opening and closing

against its will. It will occur to you
your brother is a beat-down, dubbed Bruce Lee—
his words do not match his mouth, which is moving
faster and faster. You have the fastest
brother alive.

Your brother's lips are ruined.
There is a sore in the right corner of his mouth.
My teeth hurt, he says. He will ask to go
to the IHS dentist. At a stoplight, you are forced
to look into his mouth—it is Švankmajer's rabbit hole—
you have been lost in it for the last ten years.

Pull into the restaurant parking lot.
Your brother will refuse to wear his shoes.
Judas was barefoot, he will tell you.
Judas wore sandals, you answer.
No, Jesus wore sandals, he'll argue.
Maybe one day you will laugh at this—
arguing with a meth head dressed
like a Judas effigy about Jesus's sandals.

Your brother will still itch when you are seated
at your table. He will rake his fork against his skin.
Look closer—his skin is a desert.
Half a red racer is writhing along his forearm.
A migration of tarantulas moves like a shadow
over his sunken cheeks.

Every time the waitress walks by, he licks his lips
at her. He tells you, then her, that he can taste her.
Hope she ignores him. Pretend not to hear
what he says. Also ignore the cock crowing
inside him. But if he notices you noticing,

Don't worry, he'll assure you, *The dogs will get it.*
Which dogs? You have to ask.
Then he'll point out the window at two dogs humping
in the empty lot across the way.

Go ahead. Tell him. *Those are not dogs,*
you'll say. *Those are chupacabras.*
Chupacabras are not real, he'll tell you,
brothers are. And he'll be right.

The reflection in your empty plate will speak,
Your brother is on drugs again.
You are at a dinner neither of you can eat.

Consider your brother: he is dressed
as a Judas effigy. When the waitress takes your order,
your brother will ask for a beer.
You will pour your thirty pieces of silver
onto the table and ask, *What can I get for this?*

Downhill Triolets

Sɪsʏᴘʜᴜs ᴀɴᴅ Mʏ Bʀᴏᴛʜᴇʀ

The phone rings—my brother was arrested again.
Dad hangs up, gets his old blue Chevy going, and heads to the police
    station.
It's not the first time. It's not even the second.
No one is surprised my brother was arrested again.
The guy fell on my knife, was his one-phone-call explanation.
(*He stabbed a man five times in the back* is the official accusation.)
My brother is arrested again and again. And again
our dad, our Sisyphus, pushes his old blue heart up to the station.

Gᴏᴅ, Lɪᴏɴᴇʟ Rɪᴄʜɪᴇ, ᴀɴᴅ Mʏ Bʀᴏᴛʜᴇʀ

Ring, ring, ring at 2 a.m. means meth's got my brother in the slammer
    again.
God told him, *Break into Grandma's house,* and Lionel Richie gave him that
    feeling of dancing on the ceiling.
My dad said, *At 2 a.m., God and Lionel Richie don't make good friends.*
Ring, ring, ring at 2 a.m. means meth's got my brother by the balls again.
With God in one ear and Lionel in the other, who can win?
Not my brother, so he made a meth pipe from the lightbulb and smoked
    himself reeling.
Ring, ring, ring at 2 a.m. means my brother's tweaked himself into jail
    again.
It wasn't his fault, not with God guiding his foot through the door and
    honey-voiced Lionel whispering, *Hard to keep your feet on the ground*
    with such a smooth-ass ceiling.

Tribal Cops, Geronimo, Jimi Hendrix, and My Brother

The tribal cops are in our front yard calling in on a little black radio: *I got a 10-15 for 2-6-7 and 4-15.*

The 10-15 they got is my brother, a Geronimo wannabe who thinks he's holding out. In his mind he's playing backup for Jimi—

he is an itching, bopping head full of "Fire." Mom cried, *Stop acting so crazy,* but he kept banging air drums against the windows and ripped out all the screens.

This time, *we* called the cops, and when they came we just watched—we have been here before and we know 2-6-7 and 4-15 will get him 10-15.

His eyes are escape caves torchlit by his 2-6-7 of choice: crystal methamphetamine.

Finally, he's in the back of the cop car, hands in handcuffs shiny and shaped like infinity.

Now that he's 10-15, he's kicking at the doors and security screen, a 2-6-7 fiend saying, *I got desires that burn and make me wanna 4-15.*

His tongue is flashing around his mouth like a world's fair Ferris wheel— but he's no Geronimo, Geronimo would find a way out instead of giving in so easily.

As a Consequence of My Brother Stealing All the Lightbulbs

—my parents live without light, groping,
never reading, never saying, *You are lovely.*
A broken Borges and a gouged Saint Lucia, hand in hand,
shuffling from the kitchen linoleum to the living room rug.

—my father's pants are wobbling silhouettes.
My mother is bluer than her nightgown.
One says rosaries to become a candle.
The other tries hard to be a Coleman fishing lantern
on the bank of a river twenty years away, watching
a boy he loves stab a hook through a worm.

—my parents eat matches like there's no tomorrow,
but just because they choke on today doesn't mean they aren't
proactive: They're building a funeral pyre out of their house.

— it's hard to visit.

—we are always digging each other out from an intimate
sort of rubble—I recognize some things: my brother's
high school football helmet, First Communion pin,
ceramic handprint, green plastic army men with noses
and arms chopped off, a handheld propane torch…

…so much more has been disguised by being dismantled
and fiendishly reassembled at 2 a.m.—lives, guitar amps,
the electric Virgin Mary picture with a corona that changes color,
deals with gods, the Electrolux canister vac.

—Mom and Dad snap matchsticks between their tender teeth
and I taste a green clock at the back of my throat.
The ticking is cold or sour or really a pickax.
Worry tastes so dirty when it's spread out like a banquet.

—my brother the myrrh-eater—lost fucked-up Magus,
followed the wrong star—licking his sequined lips,
which can't shine in the shade of this growing pyre.

—my dad sips gasoline through a green garden hose.
Siphons it from his own work truck so my brother can't steal it.

—my mom tries to dress the place up: riddled doilies,
the burning-heart Jesus with eyes that used to follow us
around the room until someone plucked out each bright circle.
Now my fingers slip down into the slick holes in Jesus's face.

—my mom can't wash the windows because my brother ate them.

—she knots ribbons on the wood stack,
hangs blackened spoons like wind chimes and says,
What can you expect from a pyre but a pyre?

—when I visit, I hate searching for the door—usually
my brother's boot print on my dad's ribs, once it was
a hole in my mom's chest that changed her into a sad guitar
for three years—these are more like exits than doors.
They are difficult to get through.

—the walls have been mortared with grief, dark enough
to make blindness a gift—we don't have to look each other in the eyes.

—it's crazy how loud it is inside a funeral pyre.
We don't talk much. We can't hear each other
over so much stumbling.

—when I do hear, the only thing my mom says is,
How much longer? I prefer that to what she wrote
in fluorescent paint on the ceiling last weekend:
What does he do with all the lightbulbs?

—we don't talk about crystal meth in my parents' house, particularly
since it's been converted to a funeral pyre.

—my dad quit speaking long ago. He only sings these days,
not with words, rather with small strikes and sparks.
Those quick flashes of fire that seem to satisfy
my mother's questions.

Formication

sensation of insects or snakes running over or into the skin

1. aka speed bumps

In the middle of Highway 95 I stopped my car
    while a dark cloud of tarantulas migrated
        out of the desert pulling themselves across the road—
an ebony lake of legs, black vessels launched to retrieve
    something beautiful, they climbed the jagged wash
        in such a way that I wondered if we were all living
in the wrong direction. Maybe sideways is up,
    and fucked up is up, and down is hanging over
        all our heads.
Then a semi passed me on the left.
    I can still hear the crunch. I can feel the ones that kept crawling,
        over the others, their brothers and sisters.
            Busted scabs in the road.

2. aka crank bugs

Don't tell my brother. Even though
    he's been asking, scratching for clues, picking
        at the truth. Don't tell him
there really are things skittering, creeping
    across his inner arms, moving and hot, sweating—
        We are, the Exodus. These glowing torches,
wounds that won't let us go home.

3. aka delusional parasitosis

Dope is what my dad calls it. He never says meth.
    And the dope always has my brother. *It's that dope,*
        my dad sighs, *that dope's got him.*
My dad once took us to the railroad tracks,
    gave each of his nine kids a penny to set on the rusted rails.
        My brother wanted a dollar, not a penny.
Because it's hard to turn a firstborn son away, he got it,
    shoved it down into his pocket, walked away from us.
        We placed our pennies along the rails he balanced on,
his heels squeaked against the metal, arm stretched
    out on each side. I knew then that he'd do it. He'd crucify himself
        one day, just like that day—arms nailed to a horizon of salt cedars,
            date palms, the purple mountains behind him sharp as needles.

4. aka sensation on the nerve endings

When my brother steals my dad's truck,
    my dad walks through town
        with the hoboes and train hoppers,
stray dogs, hungry accordions, the dirty-faced
    and gray-heeled girls
        who flock outside our gate like pigeons
after my brother's crumbs.
    On these days my dad drags his feet
        across my brother's skin—*Just to remind him,* my dad says,
            that I am old, I am tired,
                I am his father.

5. aka meth sores

We are too weak to say the word *intervention*.
    When my brother nods off, I write it on his arms and face in cursive
        with invisible ink— No one wants to embarrass him.
You shouldn't embarrass him, my mom says,
    Understand he's a grown man. He won't stand there
        while you embarrass him. But I'm embarrassed.
I can't understand. Why are we all just standing here
    while he tears the temple to pieces?

Mariposa Nocturna

Esta luz, este fuego que devora
Federico García Lorca

Thaïs has burst my shirt to flames, you say,
that kerosene cunt, *chingadera*.
I remind you again, you are shirtless,
sin camisa, sin vergüenza, sin, sin, sin.
Brother, I am ashamed. *Me muero de vergüenza.*
Your toothlessness. Your caved lips.
    How light flees you. *Mi hermano, mariposa nocturna.*

You march behind Thaïs anyway,
mad Macedonian prince, *Príncipe de Coger,*
with only one flip-flop clapping.
Jeers echo the alleyway, *Calle de los Perros.*
Stop this fool parade. *Estoy suplicando,*
    Find your missing shoe.

Mother's wet dresses, *los trajes vacíos,*
strung from the clotheslines above. *Un collar de fantasmas.*
How you laugh, Brother. *Ríete.*
You say, They are raining, the ladies are raining.
    Pero mi mamá llueve.

It is clearly midnight. In the sky a stampede. Elephants
licking their tusks. *Cielo de dientes.*
This hour is your temple. The waxing moon your altar.
    What you pray for stains.

Hermano de flautas y pipas. Rats are wild
at work building your shadow armor.
    Eres una sombra de ratas.

Thaïs kisses like an ember, you whisper,
already hard, with thoughts of what you will love
into blaze tonight—*que amas*—
already ash. Come morning the fields too will go
to smoke. Now, the lamp-lit moths tremble,
no longer themselves, gleaming with sex. You,
your bare foot, slicing through the city

    dark as a scythe.

Black Magic Brother

My brother's shadow flutters from his shoulders, a magician's cape.
My personal charlatan glittering in woofle dust and loaded
with gimmicks and gaffs.

A train of dirty cabooses, of once-beautiful girls,
follows my magus man like a chewed tail
helping him perform his tricks.
He calls them his *Beloveds,* his *Sim Sala Bimbos,* juggles them,
shoves them into pipes packed hot hard as cannons and *Wham Bam
Ala-Kaʒam!* whirls them to smoke.
Sometimes he vanishes their teeth then points his broken wand up
into the starry desert sky, says, *Voilà! There they are!*
and the girls giggle, revealing neon gums and purple throats.

My brother. My *mago.*
The consummate professional, he is dependable—performs daily,
nightly, in the living room, a forever-matinee, an always-late-shaman-show:
*Come one, come all! Behold the spectacle
of the Prince of Prestidigitators.*

As the main attraction (*drumroll please*) he pulls animals from a hole
in his crotch—
you thought I'd say *hat,* but you don't know my black magic brother—
and those animals love him like the first animals loved God
when He gave them names.

My brother. Our perpetual encore—
he riddles my father with red silk scarves before sawing him in half
with a steak knife. Now we have two fathers,
one who weeps anytime he hears the word *Presto!*
The other who drags his feet down the hall at night.
Neither has the stomach for steak anymore.

My mother, too, is gone somewhere
in one of the pockets of my brother's bluest tuxedo:
Abracadabrantesque!

The audience is we—we have the stubs to prove it—
and we have been here for years, in velvet chairs the color of wounds,
waiting for something to fall,
maybe the curtain, maybe the crucifix on the wall,
or, maybe the pretty white doves my brother made disappear—
Now we see them, now we don't—
will fall from his sleeves like angels—
right before our very eyes.

A Brother Named Gethsemane

Naked blue boy put down your pipe. They found your shoes in the meadow. Mom's and Dad's hearts are overripe.

Pluck that crimson orb rusted package from the branches mother's arms our tree you've chopped away at for too long with your mouth-bright ax pretty-teethed boy. Chop chop-ping. No stopping this Lost-boy-of-our-wilting-garden. Peter Pan wannabe. Peter be wanna pan. Oh don't grow up now. Don't turn away from the gapings on Mama's trunk. Watch them glow with us electric gashes wounds like hurt-lanterns you've lit. Sit Indian-legged under this moon. Hurtling shiny bullet. Hungry boy. Licking your ruby-crusted lips. Fingerpicking father's red-swelled eyes from where he cowers. A beat bush smoldering with shame. Old men should be allowed to sob in privacy. Turn up the radio. Tune in to the border stations those pirate Mexican heroin melodies. We've got to got to got to get back to that stinking garden.

Flyblown figs shimmer at you my bug-eyed boy. The glitzy-bodied flies boogie-woogie to your static grin numbing you while sexy screwworms empty you like a black hole. Ecstasy that must look pretty from inside—to core not just an apple but the entire orchard the family even the dog. Leave the shells to the crows. A field of red lampshades in the dark Garden of Myiasis. This is no cultivated haven. This is the earth riddled with a brother. The furrows are mountains. Waves of sand and we are ships wrecked. What's left of a fleet of one hundred shadows shattered and bleached. A crop gone to sticks. The honeysuckle sags with bright sour powder. We have followed the flames followed him here where all the black birds in the world have fallen like a shotgun blast to the faded ground. The vines have hardened to worms baking in the desert heat. We are at the gate shaking the gate climbing the gate clanging our cups against the gate. This is no garden. This is my brother and I need a shovel to love him.

Soirée Fantastique

Houdini arrived first, with Antigone on his arm.
Someone should have told her it was rude
to chase my brother in circles with such a shiny shovel.
She only said, *I'm building the man a funeral.*
But last I measured, my brother was still a boy.
    The doorbell chimes and chimes.
    Other guests come
in and out, snorting, mouths lathered, eyes spinning
like Spyro Gyros. They are starving, bobbing their big heads,
ready for a party. They keep saying it too, *Man, we're ready
for a party!* In their glorious twirl and dervish, none of them notices
this is no dinner party. This is a jalopy carousel—and we are
    dizzy. We are
    here to eat the horses.
There are violins playing. The violins are on fire—
they are passed around until we're all smoking. Jesus coughs,
climbs down from the cross of railroad ties above the table.
He's a regular at these carrion revelries, and it's annoying
how he turns the bread to fish, especially when we have sandwiches.
    I've never had the guts
    to ask Jesus, *Why?*
Old Houdini can't get over 'em—the hole in each of Jesus's hands—
he's smitten, and drops first a butter knife, then a candelabra through
the gaping in the right hand. He holds Jesus's left palm up to his face,
wriggles his tongue through the opening, then spits,
says, *This tastes like love.* He laughs hysterically, *Admit it Chuy,*
    between you and me,
    someone else is coming.
Antigone is back, this time with the green-handled garden spade.
Where is your brother? she demands. She doesn't realize
this is not my brother's feast—he simply set the table.

Poor Antigone. *Bury the horses, instead,* I tell her.
What will we eat then? she weeps, not knowing weeping
        isn't what it used to be, not here.
        Poor, poor, Antigone.
I look around for Houdini to get her out of here.
He's escaped. In the corner, Jesus covers his face with his hands—
each hole an oubliette—I see right through them:
None of us belong here. I'm the only one left to say it.
I ease the spade from her hand. I explain:
        We aren't here to eat, we are being eaten.
        Come, pretty girl. Let us devour our lives.

No More Cake Here

When my brother died
I worried there wasn't enough time
to deliver the one hundred invitations
I'd scribbled while on the phone with the mortuary:
Because of the short notice no need to RSVP.
Unfortunately the firemen couldn't come.
(I had hoped they'd give free rides on the truck.)
They did agree to drive by the house once
with the lights on— It was a party after all.

I put Mom and Dad in charge of balloons,
let them blow as many years of my brother's name,
jails, twenty-dollar bills, midnight phone calls,
fistfights, and ER visits as they could let go of.
The scarlet balloons zigzagged along the ceiling
like they'd been filled with helium. Mom blew up
so many that she fell asleep. She slept for ten years—
she missed the whole party.

My brothers and sisters were giddy, shredding
his stained T-shirts and raggedy pants, throwing them up
into the air like confetti.

When the clowns came in a few balloons slipped out
the front door. They seemed to know where
they were going and shrank to a fistful of red grins
at the end of our cul-de-sac. The clowns played toy bugles
until the air was scented with rotten raspberries.
They pulled scarves from Mom's ear—she slept through it.
I baked my brother's favorite cake (chocolate, white frosting).
When I counted there were ninety-nine of us in the kitchen.
We all stuck our fingers in the mixing bowl.

A few stray dogs came to the window.
I heard their stomachs and mouths growling
over the mariachi band playing in the bathroom.
(There was no room in the hallway because of the magician.)
The mariachis complained about the bathtub acoustics.
I told the dogs, *No more cake here,* and shut the window.
The fire truck came by with the sirens on. The dogs ran away.
I sliced the cake into ninety-nine pieces.

I wrapped all the electronic equipment in the house,
taped pink bows and glittery ribbons to them—
remote controls, the Polaroid, stereo, Shop-Vac,
even the motor to Dad's work truck—everything
my brother had taken apart and put back together
doing his crystal meth tricks—he'd always been
a magician of sorts.

Two mutants came to the door.
One looked almost human. They wanted
to know if my brother had willed them the pots
and pans and spoons stacked in his basement bedroom.
They said they missed my brother's cooking and did we
have any cake. *No more cake here,* I told them.
Well, what's in the piñata? they asked. I told them
God was and they ran into the desert, barefoot.
I gave Dad his slice and put Mom's in the freezer.
I brought up the pots and pans and spoons
(really, my brother was a horrible cook), banged them
together like a New Year's Day celebration.

My brother finally showed up asking why
he hadn't been invited and who baked the cake.
He told me I shouldn't smile, that this whole party was shit
because I'd imagined it all. The worst part he said was

he was still alive. The worst part he said was
he wasn't even dead. I think he's right, but maybe
the worst part is that I'm still imagining the party, maybe
the worst part is that I can still taste the cake.

III

I Watch Her Eat the Apple

She twirls it in her left hand,
a small red merry-go-round.

According to the white oval sticker,
she holds apple #4016.
I've read in some book or other
of four thousand fifteen fruits she held
before this one, each equally dizzied
by the heat in the tips of her fingers.

She twists the stem, pulls it
like the pin of a grenade, and I just know
somewhere someone is sitting alone on a porch,
bruised, opened up to their wet white ribs,
riddled by her teeth—
lucky.

With her right hand, she lifts the sticker
from the skin. Now,
the apple is more naked than any apple has been
since two bodies first touched the leaves
of ache in the garden.

Maybe her apple is McIntosh, maybe Red Delicious.
I only know it is the color of something I dreamed,
some thing I gave to her after being away
for ten thousand nights.

The apple pulses like a red bird in her hand—
she is setting the red bird free,
but the red bird will not go,
so she pulls it to her face as if to tell it a secret.

She bites, cleaving away a red wing.
The red bird sings. Yes,
she bites the apple and there is music—
a branch breaking, a ship undone by the shore,
a knife making love to a wound, the sweet scrape
of a match lighting the lamp of her mouth.

This blue world has never needed a woman
to eat an apple so badly, to destroy an apple,
to make the apple bone—
and she does it.

I watch her eat the apple,
carve it to the core, and set it, wobbling,
on the table—
a broken bell I beg to wrap my red skin around
until there is no apple,
there is only this woman
who is a city of apples,
there is only me licking the juice
from the streets of her palm.

If there is a god of fruit or things devoured,
and this is all it takes to be beautiful,
then God, please,
let her
eat another apple
tomorrow.

Toward the Amaranth Gates of War or Love

Tonight the city is glimmered.
    What's left of an August monsoon
is heat and wet. Beyond the open window,
    the streetlamp is a honey-skirted hive I could split
with my hand, my palm a pool of light.

    On the television screen, bombs like silvery bells
toll above blurred horizon—
    All I know of war is win.
What is a wall if not a thing to be pressed against?
    What is a bedroom if not an epicenter
of pillage? And what can I do with a hundred houses
    but abandon them as spent shells of desire?

The buzz of blue burning ozone molecules—
    a hypothalamus of cavalry trumpets—
call me to something—you,
    so willing to be crushed. I feel like I might die.
I lean over, kiss you sitting on the sofa
    and pretend we are lying there
stretched across that debris-dazzled desert—
    the only affliction is your mouth,
the single ache is that I cannot crawl inside you—
    the explosions are for us.

The war is nothing more
    than a reminder to go to Mass.
The tolling, your sighing.
    The bombs, a carnival of bodies, touch,
all the things we want to taste—
    an apple wedge soaked in vinegar,

a blood orange swelling like a breast—
    those beggars of teeth.

I want you like that—enough to gnash you
    into a silence made from pieces of silver.

Outside, cars rush the slick streets.
    My mouth is on your thigh—
I would die to tear just this piece of you away,
    to empty your bright dress onto the floor,
as the bombs' long, shadowy legs,
    march me toward the amaranth gates of the city.

Self-Portrait as a Chimera

I am what I have done—

A sweeping gesture to the thorn of mast jutting from my mother's spine—spine a series of narrow steps leading to the temple of her neck where the things we worship demand we hurl her heart from that height, still warm, still humming with the holy music of an organ—

We do. We do. We do and do and do.

The last wild horse leaping off a cliff at Dana Point. A hurtling god carved from red clay. Wings of wind. Two satellite eyes spiraling like coals from a long-cold fire. Dreaming of Cortés, his dirty beard and the burns it left when we kissed. Yet we kissed for years and my savage hair wove around him like a noose of smoke.

Skeletons of apples rot the gardens of Thalheim. First snow wept at the windows while I held a man's wife in my arms. I palmed her heavy breasts like loot bags. Her teeth at my throat like a pearl necklace I could break to pieces. I would break to pieces. *Dieb.*

A bandit born with masked eyes. El Maragato's thigh wound glittering like red lace. My love hidden away in a cave as I face the gallows each morning, her scent the bandanna around my face, her picture folded in the cuff of my boot.

The gravediggers and their beautiful shoulder blades smooth as shovel heads. I build and build my brother a funeral, eating the dirt along the way—queen of pica, pilferer of misery feasts—hoarding my brother like a wrecked Spanish galleon. I am more cerulean than the sea I swallow each day on the way to reaching out for him, singing his name, wearing him like a dress made of debris.

These dark rosettes name me Jaguar. These stripes are my slave dress. Black soot. Red hematite. I am filled with ink. A codex, splayed, opened, ready to be burned in the square—

I am. I am and am and am. What have I done?

Dome Riddle

Tonight I am riddled by this thick skull

this white bowling ball zipped in the sad-sack carrying case of my face,
this overwound bone jack-in-the-box,
this Orlando's zero, Oaxacan offering: *cabeza locada, calavera azucarada,*
    clavo jodido, cenote of Mnemosyne,
this sticky-sweet guilt hive, *piedra blanca del rio oscuro,*
this small-town medical mania dispensary, prescribed cranium pill,
this electric blue tom-tom drum ticking like an Acme bomb, hypnotized
    explosive device, pensive general, scalp-strapped warrior, soldier
    with a loaded God complex,
this Hotchkiss-obliterated headdress, Gatling-lit labyrinth,
this memory grenade, death epithet, death epitaph, mound of *momento*
    mori,
this twenty-two-part talisman wearing a skirt of breasts, giant ball of
    masa,
this god patella in the long leg of my torso, zoo of canines and Blake's
    tygers,
this red-skinned apple, lamp illuminated by teeth, gang of grin, spitwad
    of scheme,
this jawbone of an ass, smiling sliver of smite, David's rock striking the
    Goliath of my body,
this Library of Babel, homegrown Golgotha, nostalgia menagerie, melon
    festival,
this language mausoleum: *chuksanych iraavtahanm, 'avi kwa'anyay,*
    sumach nyamasav,
this hidden glacier hungry for a taste of titanic flesh,
this pleasure altar, French-kiss sweatshop, abacus of one-night stands,
    hippocampus whorehouse, oubliette of regret,
this church of tongue, chapel of vengeance, cathedral of thought, bone
    dome of despair, *plaza del toro y pensamientos,*

this museum of tribal dentistry, commodity cranium cupboard, petrified
 dream catcher,
this sun-ruined basketball I haul—rotted gray along the seams—perpetual
 missed shot,
this insomnia podium, little bowl in a big fish, brain amphitheater, girl in
 the moon,
this 3 a.m. war bell, *duende* vision prison,
this single-scoop vanilla head rush, thunder head, fastball, lightning rod,
this mad scientist in a white lab helmet, ghost of Smoking Mirror,
this coyote beacon, calcium corral of pale perlino ponies,
this desert seed I am root to, night-blooming cereus, gourd gone rattle,
this Halloween crown, hat rack, worry contraption, Rimbaud's drunken
 boat, blazing chandelier, *casa de relámpago,*
this coliseum *venatio*: Borges's other tiger licking the empty shell of
 Lorca's white *tortuga,*
this underdressed godhead, forever-hatching egg, this mug again and
 again at my lips,

and all this because tonight I imagined you sleeping with her
the way we once slept—as intimate as a jaw, maxilla and mandible hot,
in the skin—in love, our heads almost touching.

I Lean Out the Window and She Nods Off in Bed, the Needle Gently Rocking on the Bedside Table

While she sleeps, I paint
Valencia oranges across her skin,
seven times the color orange,
a bright tree glittering the limestone grotto of her clavicle—
heaving bonfires pulsing each pale limb
like Nero's condemned heretics sparking along Via Appia.

A small stream of Prussian blue I've trickled
down her bicep. A fat red nasturtium
eddies her inner elbow.

Against her swollen palms,
I've brushed glowing halves of avocados
lamping like bell-hipped women in ecstasy.

A wounded Saint Teresa sketched to each breast.

Her navel is a charcoal bowl of figs,
all stem thick with sour milk and gowned
in taffeta the color of bruises.

This to offer up with our flophouse prayers—

God created us with absence
in our hands, but we will not return that way.
Not now, when we are both so capable of growing full
on banquets embroidered by Lorca's gypsy nun.

She sleeps, gone to the needle's gentle rocking,
and I lean out the window, a Horus
drunk on my own scent
and midnight's slow drip of stars.

She has always been more orchard than loved,
I, more bite than mouth.

So much is empty in this hour—
the spoon, still warm, lost in the sheets,
the candle's yellow-white thorn of flame,
a vanishing ribbon of jade smoke,
and night, open as autumn's unfilled basket
as the locusts feast the field.

Monday Aubade

with a line from Rimbaud

To be next to you again,

to feel the knob of your pelvic bone,
the door of your hip opening
to a room of light
where a fuchsia blouse hangs
in the closet of a conch shell,
the silhouette of a single red-mouthed bell;

to shut my eyes one more night

on the delta of shadows
between your shoulder blades—
mysterious wings tethered inside
the pale cage of your body—run through
by Lorca's horn of moonlight,
strange unicorn loose along the dim streets
separating our skins;

to be still again knowing

the bow of your spine, the arc of your torso—
a widening road to an alabaster mountain,
a secret path to a cliff overlooking a sea
salt-heavy and laced in foam, a caravel
crushing the swells, parting each
like blue-skirted thighs—lay before me,
another New World shore the gods
have chained me to;

to have you a last time, at last, a touch away,

but then, to not reach out
because my hands are dressed in scarves of smoke;

to lie silent at your side,

an ember more brilliant with each yellow breath,
glowing and dying and dying again,
dreaming a mesquite forest I once stripped to fire
before the sky went ash, undid its dark ribbons,
and bent to the ground, grief-ruined,

as I watch you from the window—
in this city, the city of you, where I am a beggar—
    the Dawns are heartbreaking.

When the Beloved Asks, "What Would You Do if You Woke Up and I Was a Shark?"

My lover doesn't realize that I've contemplated this scenario,
fingered it like the smooth inner iridescence of a nautilus shell
in the shadow-long waters of many 2 a.m.s—drunk on the brine

of shoulder blades, those pale horns of shore I am wrecked upon,
my mind treading the wine-dark waves of luxuria's tempests—
as a matter of preparedness, and because I do not sleep for fear

of such things or even other things—I've read that the ocean
is a large pot of Apocalypse soup soon to boil over with our sins—
but a thing is a thing, especially if it's a 420-million-year-old beast,

especially if you have wronged so many as I. Beauty, it is simple,
more simple than a beloved can imagine: I wouldn't fight, not kick,
flail, not carry on like one driven mad by the black neoprene wetsuit

of death, not like sad-mouthed, despair-eyed albacore or blubbery
pinnipeds, wouldn't rage the city's flickering streets of ampullae
of Lorenzini, nor slug my ferocious, streamlined lover's titanium

white nose, that bull's-eye of cartilage, no, I wouldn't prolong it.
Instead, I'd place my head onto that dark altar of jaws, prostrated
pilgrim at Melville's glittering gates, climb into that mysterious

window starred with teeth—the one lit room in the charnel house.
I, at once mariner, at once pirate, would navigate my want by those
throbbing constellations. I'd wear those jaws like a toothy cilice,

slip into the glitzy red gown of penance, and it would be no different
from what I do each day—voyaging the salt-sharp sea of your body,
sometimes mooring the ports or sighting the sextant, then mending

the purple sails and hoisting the masts before being bound to them. Be-loved, *is* loved, what you cannot know is I am overboard for this metamorphosis, ready to be raptured to that mouth, reduced to a swell of wet clothes, as you roll back your eyes and drag me into the fathoms.

Lorca's Red Dresses

Tonight, after reading Lorca's *Cante jondo,* I'm ready, dressed
for the procession, for Jesus's wounds, the mob's red dresses.

The Gitana's savage hair charges the night, *nocturno de guerra,* battle-
field of a thousand and one bulls. Their weapons: violent red dresses.

Santa Teresa, *torera,* sacrificed her body to the pale horns. A First
Confession: the split fruit made my thighs buck under my red dress.

What hips! *Péndulos.* And breasts! Clocks adorning the dim hall-
ways of kiss—there is chiming and hands beneath the red dress.

Men crouch, crotches tremulous in the creaking ribcage of a horse.
Who hasn't beat at the gates of Troy for a taste of Helen's red dress?

Cherries dazzle the branches, merciless vermilion gods.
My tongue's a heretic, prostrated. My heart's a red dress.

El colibrí atormentado thrummed honeysuckle's orange guitar to inferno.
Azaleas wept jealously, bruised knees mourning September's red dresses.

The soldiers' guns were blue tapers. An olive tree, a requiem. Silver
flies riddled the sky. Three men and a poet slept hard in red dresses.

Yesterday's pains scar over. The body is canvas—Picasso's
Guernica: open palms, questions, the lamp's faded red dress.

We are black poplars at the foot of Sacromonte. They mistake
salt for *azúcar,* these ants devouring us like magic red dresses.

India, give in to the shells chafing your shadowy thighs and belly
while *Lucía Martínez* builds your evening pyre, your final red dress.

Of Course She Looked Back

You would have, too.
From that distance the shivering city
fit in the palm of her hand
like she owned it.

She could've blown the whole thing—
markets, dance halls, hookah bars—
sent the city and its hundred harems
tumbling across the desert
like a kiss. She had to look back.

When she did she saw
pigeons glinting like debris above
ruined rooftops. Towers swaying.
Women in broken skirts
strewn along burned-out streets
like busted red bells.

The noise was something else—
dogs wept, roosters howled, children
and guitars popped like kernels of corn
feeding the twisting blaze.

She wondered had she unplugged
the coffeepot? The iron?
Was the oven off?
Her husband uttered, *Keep going.*
Whispered, *Stay the course,* or
Baby, forget about it. She couldn't.

Now a bursting garden of fire
the city bloomed to flame after flame
like hot fruit in a persimmon orchard.

Someone thirsty asked for water.
Someone scared asked to pray.
Her daughters or the crooked-legged angel,
maybe. Dark thighs of smoke opened
to the sky. She meant to look
away, but the sting in her eyes,
the taste devouring her tongue,
and the neighbors begging her name.

Apotheosis of Kiss

I dipped my fingers in the candle wax at church—
white votives shivered in red glass

at the foot of la Virgen's gown—
glowing green-gold.

The fever was fast—
my body ablaze,

I pulled back.
Pale silk curved on each fingertip—

peeling it away was like small gasps.
The candles flickered—

open mouths begging.
Heretics banged at the double door.

Charismatics paraded the aisles,
twirling tapers, flinging Sunday hats.

The Rapture came and went, left
me, the choir's bright robes,

collection baskets like broken tambourines—
What poverty, to never know,

to never slide over the lip of a candle
toward flame—raving to touch

her bare brown toes.

Orange Alert

There are certain words
you can't say in airports—
words that mean bomb, blow up, jihad,
hijack, terrorist, terrorism, terrorize,
terrific fucking terror.
        And words like *orange*—
small citrus grenades,
laced with steel seeds, rinds lined
with anthrax.
        Security cameras scan and scrutinize
Californians. Floridians
are profiled, picked for full-body
fondlings—everyone knows Florida
is the Axis of Oranges.
        Loudspeakers announce:
All passengers' navels
must be covered or checked in baggage.
Congress is considering mandatory
navelectomies.
Orange Alert paranoia eats away
at the nation like a very hungry caterpillar.
        The Mexicans, known agents of oranges,
are scared—taking to the streets, picketing,
fighting for *naranjas* as if they were their own
corazones. They don't understand—
We don't fly, they say. *If we want to travel*
we borrow Tía Silvi's minivan.
        Pamphlets flutter from the sky
telling how to tell
if someone's a terrorist: They tell jokes
with punch lines like:

Orange you glad I didn't say banana?
    Women with B cups, men with certain-
sized crotches, even those with
man-boobs, are squeezed, bobbled in search
of forbidden fruits—questioned
about stowed-away pomelos, tangelos,
sun-kissed improvised explosive devices,
quarters of tart dynamite.
    Orchards are napalmed.
Homeland Security says, *Convert them all*
        to parking lots. Go, men! Go!
We're out for blood oranges.
    Orange Aide to Third World fruit stands
was canceled.
The U.N. expunged
the Oranges for Oil campaign.
It doesn't stop there—
    patriot posses mow down highway cones,
the DOT revolted and wrecked their fleets
of clementine-colored trucks,
school crossing guards are mauled in their tangy vests—
beaten with Walk signs
by packs of anti-mandarin kindergarteners.
O.J. Simpson's in jail.
    Tropicana sold out to V8.
Orange County is a mere smudge
in the West Coast sky.
    Halloween was banned—
Jehovah's Witnesses shake their heads
saying, *We told you so.*
In the haze of this early winter,
blue flames engulf the cities.

Wait—what's that you say?
We've been bumped to red alert?
But that's like apples and oranges.

The Elephants

Hast thou not seen how thy Lord dealt with the
possessors of the elephant?

al-Fil, sura 105, Qur'an

My brother still hears the tanks
    when he is angry—they rumble like a herd of hot green
        elephants over the plowed streets inside him, crash through

the white oleanders lining my parents' yard
    during family barbecues, great scarred ears flapping, commanding
        a dust storm that shakes blooms from the stalks like wrecked stars.

One thousand and one sleepless nights
    bulge their thick skulls, gross elephant boots pummel
        ice chests, the long barrels of their trunks crush cans of cheap beer

and soda pop in quick, sparkling bursts of froth,
    and the meat on the grill goes to debris in the flames
        while the rest of us cower beneath lawn chairs.

When the tusked animals in my brother's miserable eyes
    finally fall asleep standing up, I find the nerve to ask him
        what they sound like, and he tells me, *It's no hat dance,*

and says that unless I've felt the bright beaks of ancient Stymphalian birds,
    unless I've felt the color red raining from Heaven and marching
        in my veins, I'll never know the sound of war.

But I do know that since my brother's been back,
    orange clouds hang above him like fruit made of smoke,
        and he sways in trancelike pachyderm rhythm

to the sweet tings of death music circling

    circling his head like an explosion of bluebottle flies

        haloing him—*I'm no saint,* he sighs, flicking each one away.

He doesn't sit in chairs anymore and is always on his feet,

    hovering by the window, peeking out the door, *Because,*

        he explains, *everyone is the enemy, even you, even me.*

The heat from guns he'll never let go

    rises up from his fists like a desert mirage, blurring

        everything he tries to touch or hold— If we cry

when his hands disappear like that, he laughs,

    Those hands, he tells us, *those little Frankensteins*

    were never my friends.

But before all this, I waited for him

    as he floated down the airport escalator in his camouflage BDUs.

        An army-issued duffel bag dangled from his shoulders—

hot green elephants,

    their arsenal of memory, rocking inside.

        He was home. He was gone.

Why I Don't Mention Flowers When Conversations with My Brother Reach Uncomfortable Silences

> *Forgive me, distant wars, for bringing*
> *flowers home.*
>
> Wisława Szymborska

In the Kashmir mountains,
my brother shot many men,
blew skulls from brown skins,
dyed white desert sand crimson.

What is there to say to a man
who has traversed such a world,
whose hands and eyes have
betrayed him?

Were there flowers there? I asked.

This is what he told me:

In a village, many men
wrapped a woman in a sheet.
She didn't struggle.
Her bare feet dragged in the dirt.

They laid her in the road
and stoned her.

The first man was her father.
He threw two stones in a row.
Her brother had filled his pockets
with stones on the way there.

The crowd was a hive
of disturbed bees. The volley
of stones against her body
drowned out her moans.

Blood burst through the sheet
like a patch of violets,
a hundred roses in bloom.

The Beauty of a Busted Fruit

When we were children, we traced our knees,
shins, and elbows for the slightest hint of wound,
searched them for any sad red-blue scab marking us
both victim and survivor.

All this before we knew that some wounds can't heal,
before we knew the jagged scars of Great-Grandmother's
amputated legs, the way a rock can split a man's head
open to its red syrup, like a watermelon, the way a brother
can pick at his skin for snakes and spiders only he can see.

Maybe you have grown out of yours—
maybe you no longer haul those wounds with you
onto every bus, through the side streets of a new town,
maybe you have never set them rocking in the lamplight
on a nightstand beside a stranger's bed, carrying your hurts
like two cracked pomegranates, because you haven't learned
to see the beauty of a busted fruit, the bright stain it will leave
on your lips, the way it will make people want to kiss you.

Love Potion 2012

Buzzards
             able oarsmen
                          drag black oars
                                       dripping foam
commandeering this rat-gilded vessel and hull
             full with ghosts
                          shoving dead elephants across the menagerie deck
                                       overboard

The smooth thick bones float
             end over end wandering jagged ocean floor—

             Patellae shifting like dandelion seed   A Halloween mask
             of pelvic bone roams a neighborhood in a dream   Silvered
             horseshoes of mandibles canter spitting sand

             —tumbling skeletons of magnolia petals smitten by July
             wind—

but none of this before the wrecked bodies
             turn sponge and tusk

swell even as the gray flesh is carried
             sucked away to the bellies of lamprey
                          Crustacea dressed in teeth

I am a fool

This is no sea   Clouds not reef not stone
             This heavy coat is atmosphere The vultures
                          dredge cast-iron ladles Not oars

Taste hearts and turnips
        in their throats Sky is cauldron
           How they stir
                this awful elixir Gods and bombs

zagging through the air like coins
        down an empty well No eye of newt
           No hair of bezoar Mandrake either
                Just the willingness to hold
                      to lie

quiet as a carcass

A Wild Life Zoo

sleep is good, better is death

Heinrich Heine, "Morphine"

I watched a lion eat a man like a piece of fruit, peel tendons from fascia
like pith from rind, then lick the sweet meat from its hard core of bones.
The man had earned this feast and his own deliciousness by ringing a stick
against the lion's cage, calling out, *Here, Kitty Kitty, Meow!*

With one swipe of a paw much like a catcher's mitt with fangs, the lion
pulled the man into the cage, rattling his skeleton against the metal bars.

The lion didn't want to do it—
He didn't want to eat the man like a piece of fruit, and he told the crowd
this: *I only wanted some goddamn sleep.* The crowd had trouble believing
the words sliding out of the lion's mouth, a mouth the size of a cathedral
with a vaulted ceiling, maxilla and mandible each like a flying buttress.
They believed the lion even less when they saw that one or two of his
words had been impaled on his teeth, which were pointed and lined up in
a semicircle like large pink wigwams at a war party. The crowd scattered,
fleeing to the pagoda bridge over the koi pond and the tinted windows
of the humid reptile house.

But, I believed the lion—
I had seen him yawn. I had fallen in love with that yawn and my thighs
panged just thinking about laying my head inside that wet dark bed
of jaws. So, I stayed, despite the man glittering and oozing on the ground
like a mortal wound.

About the time the lion burped up the man's jeans, now as shredded as
a blue grass skirt, a jeep of twelve zoo workers screeched around the
rhino exhibit in SWAT gear and khaki shorts—to rescue the man who
was crumpled on the floor like a red dress that had too many drinks—

their tranquilizer guns shone like Saint Michael's swords, and they each held a handful of dope-filled darts with neon pink feathers at the ends.

The lion paid this Zoo Crusade little attention and burped up the man's asshole next. He looked at me and said, *I hate assholes.* (Seven darts hit him at once, causing him to wince.) *But,* the lion continued, *the eyes…you can't beat those salty, olivelike eyes.* An ear dangled like a yo-yo from his goatee as he shook his massive rock-star hair and stumbled off toward a shallow cave at the back of his cage, dragging his tail behind him like a medieval flail. All seven darts jangled and clicked from his flanks like a tambourine made of pink aloe flowers. The Zoo Delta Force Team followed behind him, stepping in the thick tracks his heavy tail had made. The crowd, now hiding out like two separate groups of bandits, was wary of the animals they found themselves near at that particular moment: the gaping gobs of the electric koi beneath the surface of the flotsamed pond, opening and closing their lips in a song shaped like skulls, and the agile maws of the boa constrictors and pythons, unhinging and resetting their jaws like basement doors. But I believed the lion and rang my bowl against the cage to let them know.

About the Author

Natalie Diaz grew up in the Fort Mojave Indian Village in Needles, California, on the banks of the Colorado River. She is Mojave and an enrolled member of the Gila River Indian Community. After playing professional basketball in Europe and Asia for several years, she completed an MFA in poetry and fiction from Old Dominion University in 2007. She currently lives in Mohave Valley, Arizona, and directs a language revitalization program at Fort Mojave, her home reservation. There she works with the last Elder speakers of the Mojave language.

Lannan Literary Selections

For two decades Lannan Foundation has supported the publication and distribution of exceptional literary works. Copper Canyon Press gratefully acknowledges their support.

LANNAN LITERARY SELECTIONS 2012

Matthew Dickman and Michael Dickman, *50 American Plays*

Michael McGriff, *Home Burial*

Tung Hui-Hu, *Greenhouses, Lighthouses*

James Arthur, *Charms Against Lightning*

Natalie Diaz, *When My Brother Was an Aztec*

RECENT LANNAN LITERARY SELECTIONS FROM COPPER CANYON PRESS

Michael Dickman, *Flies*

Laura Kasischke, *Space, In Chains*

Deborah Landau, *The Last Usable Hour*

Sarah Lindsay, *Twigs and Knucklebones*

Heather McHugh, *Upgraded to Serious*

W.S. Merwin, *Migration: New & Selected Poems*

Valzhyna Mort, *Collected Body*

Taha Muhammad Ali, *So What: New & Selected Poems, 1971-2005,* translated by Peter Cole, Yahya Hijazi, and Gabriel Levin

Lucia Perillo, *Inseminating the Elephant*

Ruth Stone, *In the Next Galaxy*

John Taggart, *Is Music: Selected Poems*

Jean Valentine, *Break the Glass*

C.D. Wright, *One Big Self: An Investigation*

Dean Young, *Fall Higher*

For a complete list of Lannan Literary Selections from Copper Canyon Press, please visit Partners on our Web site: www.coppercanyonpress.org

Since 1972, Copper Canyon Press has fostered the work of emerging, established, and world-renowned poets for an expanding audience. The Press thrives with the generous patronage of readers, writers, booksellers, librarians, teachers, students, and funders — everyone who shares the belief that poetry is vital to language and living.

MAJOR SUPPORT HAS BEEN PROVIDED BY:

The Paul G. Allen Family Foundation

Amazon.com

Anonymous

Arcadia Fund

John Branch

Diana and Jay Broze

Beroz Ferrell & The Point, LLC

Mimi Gardner Gates

Golden Lasso, LLC

Gull Industries, Inc.
on behalf of William and Ruth True

Carolyn and Robert Hedin

Lannan Foundation

Rhoady and Jeanne Marie Lee

National Endowment for the Arts

New Mexico Community Foundation

Penny and Jerry Peabody

Joseph C. Roberts

Cynthia Lovelace Sears and Frank Buxton

Washington State Arts Commission

Charles and Barbara Wright

Generous support of this publication has been made in memory of Pat Curran, an esteemed member of the arts and poetry community.

To learn more about underwriting Copper Canyon Press titles, please call 360-385-4925 ext. 103

The pressmark for Copper Canyon Press
suggests entrance, connection, and interaction
while holding at its center
an attentive, dynamic space for poetry.

The poems are set in Fournier.
Book design and composition by Phil Kovacevich.